Sunset in the Morning

Sunset in the Morning

Poems by
Robert Sparago

PRECOCITY PRESS

Published by Precocity Press, Venice, CA
Cover Design: Tim Kummerow
Book Design: Susan Shankin
Photography: Robert Sparago

ISBN: 978-1-7373539-4-2

Nancy 'The Hoffer' Hoff
(July 7, 1949–September 11, 2019)

Always lending a loving hand
when my head got buried in the sand

ROSECRANS AVE.

Contents

Over an Eighteen Month Span

To the bus drivers,
(except one, in my hometown, go figure)
train conductors, and all the kind folk

Albuquerque, NM	Carson City, NV
Antelope Acres, CA	Century City, CA
Baton Rouge, LA	Culver City, CA
Berkeley, CA	Denver, CO
California 126	Flagstaff, AZ

Gardnerville, NV
'Hacienda'
Hawthorne, CA
Hollywood, CA
Hollywood Hills
Lake Hughes, CA
Lake Oswego, OR
Lake Tahoe, NV
Las Vegas, NV
Los Angeles, CA
LSU
Malibu
Manhattan Beach, CA
Manhattan Beach Pier
Martinez, CA
Mesa, AZ
New Orleans, LA
New York City
Northridge, CA
Northridge Park
Oakland, CA
Onalaska,WA
Oregon City, OR
Oxnard, CA
Pacific Coast Highway
Palmdale, CA
Palos Verdes, CA
Park City, UT

Phoenix, AZ
Portland, OR
Port Richmond, CA
Quartz Hill, CA
Rancho Cucamonga, CA
Rancho Relaxo
Redondo Beach, CA
Richmond, VA
Route 23
San Fernando Valley
Santa Barbara, CA
Santa Fe, NM
Santa Monica, CA
Savannah, GA
Summerlin, NV
UCLA
Valencia, CA
Venice, CA
Venice Beach Pier
Ventura, CA
Virginia City, NV
Truckee, NV
Wellington, NV
West Hollywood, CA
Westwood, CA
Winslow, AZ
And everywhere in between

Never Forever Young

Tie Stick was our scene at fifteen
Hangin' ten on some random block
Vega windows rolled up tight
Foreigner's *Juke Box Hero*
Cranking through one speaker door
The other broken on the floor
Never a bore at Carl's Toy Store
In heaven with a few bucks at 7-Eleven
Munchin' down Shakey's Bunch of Lunch
Skateboarding to Thrifty's for a Triple Scoop
    Chocolate Malted Crunch

Saturday mornings after Super Friends
Meet my grandpop
At the counter-top
At Dyle's Coffee Shop
The hostess was definitely the mostess
Checkin' out her Raquel Welch legs
Eating my overcooked scrambled eggs

Weekdays waking up to *Let's Make a Deal*'s
    lovely Carol Merrill
Dig into the candy barrels at Farrell's
Sometimes indulging in a Zoo with the Jew crew
Kick it with Spicoli for the umpteenth time
    at the Peppertree 3
Sneaking in for free
Hours of air hockey at Malibu Grand Prix

Chillin' on the hometown swings after dusk
Gazing at poetry in motion cutting through the
    tennis courts
Our summer French kisses wearing colorful
    tight dolphin shorts
Matching their flip flops with their tube tops

Often climb the back wall to get a peek at
    Oakridge Ranch
Never did get a glance at the movie star or his
    fancy car
Mom got a wink with a bright light red carpet
    smile on aisle 4 at Dale's Grocery Store

Too many untalented clowns today in
    Tinsel Town
You're less than subpar you get a star
They lost their Audrey Hepburn grace
In Hollywood's once exclusive space

Weeknights I'd listen to Carson on the portable
    black and white
Stare at those blank posters on the walls
Wait for the late-night verbal brawls
Inconsistent consistent dysfunction took its toll
    on the adolescent soul
Did not achieve my lifetime goal

For better or for worse
Never forever young
Just around the bend
Came youth to a quick end
Still lovin' me some Sean Penn

Olive Eyes

No college degree
And a lonely forty-three smashing into a beaten
    down sunrise after exiting a grimy
    Greyhound station
Need to wash off those not so playful romper
    room lies in this one class clown town
She wasn't even a Cracker Jack prize
Should go ocean deep
Next time I dive into a brand spankin' new set
    of eyes

Mind tends to drift heading up the seedy alley
Thinking about mortality
A soul-searching totality
No fan of everyday reality

Bomber jacket and the heart and soul
Falling into a non-wishing well bottomless
    watering hole
Where forgotten dreams comfortably sit
    on drunken stools

Her olive eyes and thirties trapped pouring
    drinks to dirty drunks and hostile punks
Not listening to shoeless drifters in funks

She lights a smoke
I light my own
Pours me a 12 ounce Pabst on tap
Talk my gap of rap
Wears her wedding band with lost years
And too many tears after saying "I do"
    on a broken-down merry-go-round
Dressed in an innocent diamond white
    bridal gown

Just might stick around this non-jukebox joint
Continue my Grand Canyon free fall
Right into an episode of Better Call Saul
Maybe get my autographed picture on the life-
less wall

Unlucky Horse Shoes

Hitching post and bat wing doors
Sawdust on the floor
Decades of baggage taking in a Colt 45 brunch
And a few smokes with the country folk at
    Jenson's Saloon
Unlucky Horse Shoes jammin' on haystacks
Kicks into *Who'll Stop The Rain*

Vans always Denny's choice brand
But the nowhere path not always grand
The early afternoon slowly fades
The band is almost done
But the windmill begins to hum

Passing by Pebble Stone Nursery
Underneath the peace sign
    on the side of the barn
Grace knits her yarn
    with her farmland charm

A cutie pie mom sporting a Hops baseball cap
And her little rascals wave on by
    crusin' a Quad what a cool family squad

Scooter and Roo skateboard on through
Chance chases the lost leaves
Blowing down between the big leaf maple trees

Sitting on a broken down porch step
His cross on her chest
Cyndie Lou sips her daily 7n7's
Gazing at his '79 Corvette
Waiting for fate for one last date
With her high school soulmate
Number 44 was so handsomely bright
Under those Friday Night Lights

Never the same gorgeous day hanging
     in postcard *Mayberry USA*
Behind the infamous white picket fence
All in overalls eating Hershey Bars
Drinking lemonade from Mason Jars
Nice to see young smiles
Not around the TV dial

Jim and Louise raking the leaves
    with their lifetime country mile smile
Lucky to get a glance
At their dance of old school romance

Off exit 59 at Ms. Beesley's Burgers
Accompanied by a sleepless pen
And the sound of a crowded train
Denny's writing can't stop the rain
But heals those childhood pains

He and Orange Crush head on out
She keeps his dark tears comfort and close
As they listen to Springsteen's old school rock
Missing her early bird French kisses
Thinking en route to go see Scout

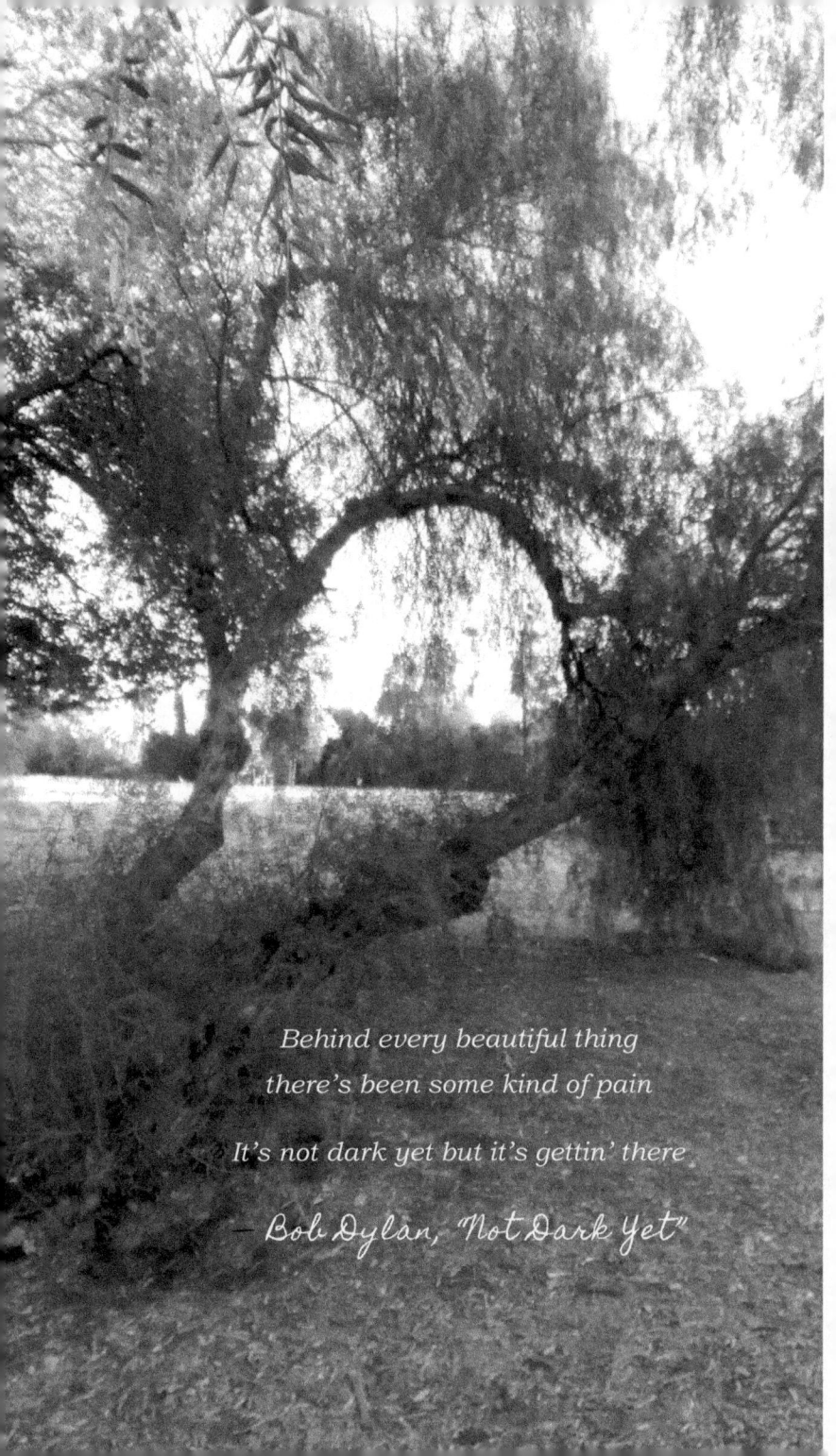

Behind every beautiful thing
there's been some kind of pain

It's not dark yet but it's gettin' there

— Bob Dylan, "Not Dark Yet"

Jade

Thru the halls of junior high
Colorful Down Jackets
    strutting past the mint green lockers
Pee Chee folders in hand
Aerosmith's *Walk This Way*
    jammin' in our dazed heads
We didn't have a care
Not even during Truth or Dare

Bus 33 took us to our secret clubhouse
No ticket stubs
No popcorn popping
No Raisinets
No fountain drink
Just a silent projector
A sticky floor
One movie poster on the wall ready to fall
We'd kiss in the dusty balcony
Like we've never done before
We kept going back for more

Over the grounds of Devonshire Downs
A 9th grade graduation flare in the air
Our classmates' voice gracefully singing
    the Carpenters' *We've Only Just Begun*
Jade and I made a pinky promise
Hold hands together and forever
But time does not like to stay the same
Jade moved away the following May
My second worst day

Sadness and madness filled her twenties
Never the proper tender loving and care
Heard Jade would be okay
Didn't turn out that way

On the boarded-up lifeguard station
A dude blowin' his horn
    in his one man sax band
I see an image of the late Clarence Clemons
Leaning on Jersey's beloved son
Mr. Born to Run

Mind shifts to Jade's autumn eyes
Her cut-off shorts and tan legs
Feet snuggled in the sand
Powder blue sandals in hand

My mid-afternoon darkness takes me to
    no longer once was
Burt Reynolds and Cybill Shepard
On that movie poster on the wall ready to fall

Quietly alone waiting for Bus 33
Rain drops and tear drops are on their way
The saxophone continues to play

No Curtain Call

Long gone the elegance
Not enough script intelligence
Win the gold statue
If the monkey suit country club schlub
    pays the big bucks for ads and billboards
Too many Hollywood hacks
No more old school Carlin funny
Whatever happened to the Playboy Bunny

Inside the underground grungy section of town
Where the city angels even come around
    not to be found
No searchlights and red carpet after
    party celebrations here
Just real LA tears
Dropping on Roy's heartaches and fears

Countless LA starless falls
No life changing phone call
The constant rejection
Knock down bouts with depression
Swept him off Snagglepuss's famous
    exit stage left
Delivered him back unscripted to his hometown
    of Hackensack

Town crony wasting usual time on dead end
    corner off Route 4
Gives Roy smack not having a career
    like the one and only Jack
Too late to start the blame game
Hung over from cheap booze
Wishing he was Tom Cruise
Not to end up à la Howard Hughes

Lying on a buddy's basement floor
Zero glamour or a single camera with
   no Houdini escape door
Rain drops knocking late
Keeping the manic hours wide awake
The curtain impatiently waits
Before his Tony award-winning last take

Floating down stream
From the soundless waterfall
Steppenwolf's *Magic Carpet Ride*
Lands in for its first verse
Roy nails his last line
Disappears like the rabbit in the top hat
But won't be reappearing for the applause
Moving on to his second act
The curtain drops
His screen turns black

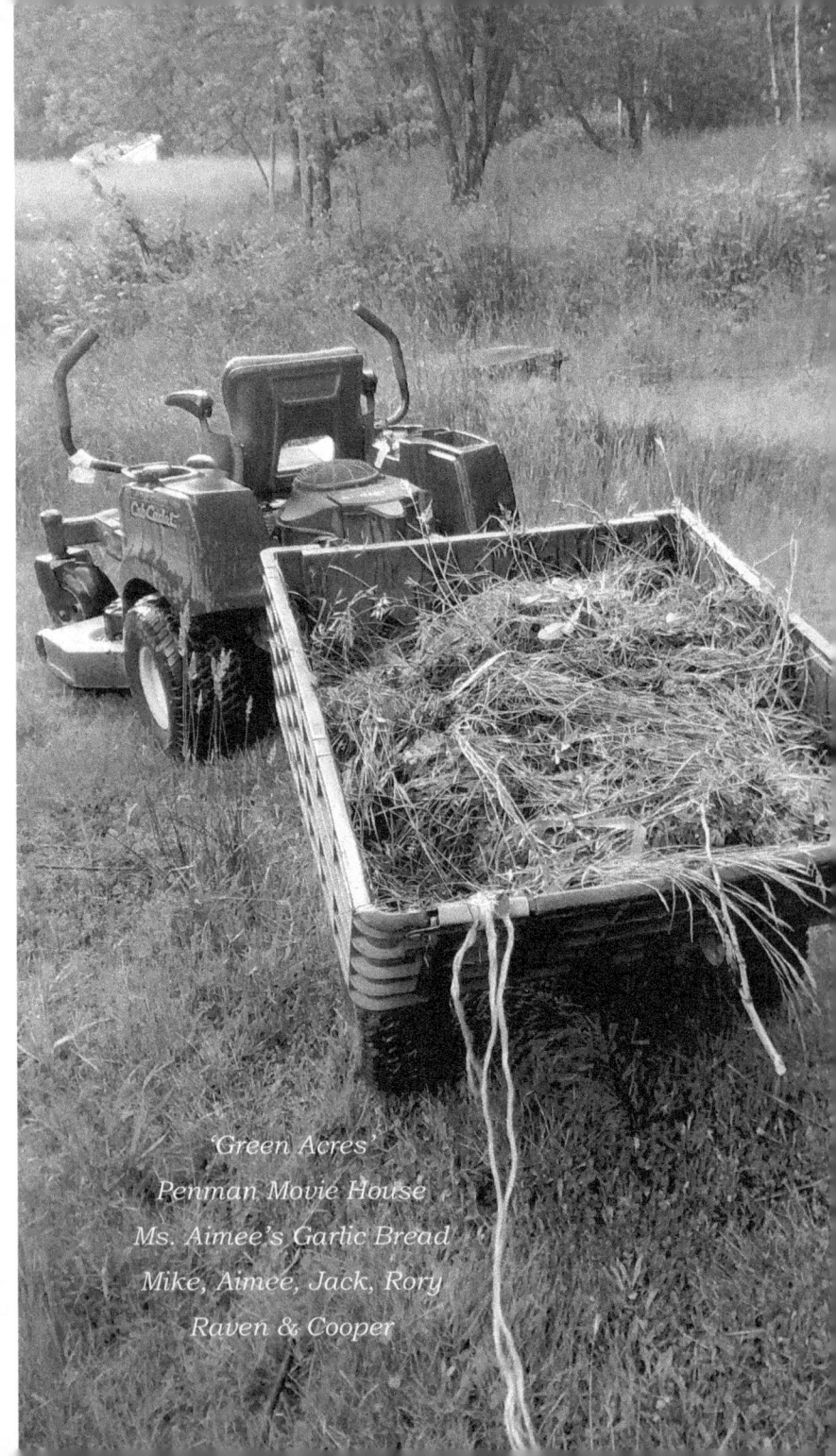

'Green Acres'
Penman Movie House
Ms. Aimee's Garlic Bread
Mike, Aimee, Jack, Rory
Raven & Cooper

Two Cherries on Top

The hostess Diner welcome
Lots of main street chatter
Mixing in the waffle batter
A petite gal in scuffed up Doc Martens
Slips on her pink John Deere beanie cap
Pays the breakfast bill
Teenagers get their flapjacks fill
An elder deep into his morning read
Love bugs dig into a Hot Fudge Sundae
Extra whip cream two cherries on top
Missing our early romantic highs
And a piece of chocolate cream pie

Never did hear someone say life is fair
    as she pours me a second cup
      and gives me the waitress's dime a dozen
      dreams are long gone smile

I soon exit Sunny Side Up
Dally into the 88th Annual Tickle Creek
    Christmas Tree Lighting
Head towards the Double Cinema no more

Christmas Eve snowflakes on our first date
Holding hands so youthfully
    and truthfully tight
Relishing in a box of Hot Tamales
Belly laughing at a cool cat named Axel Foley
And a dude named Jeff Spicoli
Molly's laugh stealing scenes from
    the old movie screen

She's the one and only Eyes of blue
Fan of Winnie the Pooh
And the lovable Mr. Magoo
If one of us had the flu
Still stuck together like crazy glue
Some nights a tasty summer brew
Listening to our guy Eddie Vedder
As we read our old college love letters

Travel the back open dirt roads
Behind the windshield of Ole Blue
And Sirius XM Channel 22
Singing to those Country soft baby blues

A silent yawn from the tired afternoon sun
Brings me right on course for
    my drink of choice
Behind the rotted-out back picket fence
The fox does her neighborly trot
We stare and share a forget everything moment
My heart stays with her though
    no longer in sight
Did the same on that pitch-dark starless
    fall autumn night
When Molly left on Heaven's 143 flight

Our perfect knot will never untie
"Until death do us part" so untrue
We still stick together like crazy glue

No Pedal to the Metal

As a hungover Hollywood Hills rises
Rain drops
And Gene Kelly tap dancing through Sunset
    and Vine
Jackson Browne playing in the background
Doyle's fingertips don't miss a beat on the
    steering wheel of his Triple Black 66

He passes the Cat and Fiddle
Heads on over to The Griddle
Tells the sleepy waitress a classic riddle
She gives him a half of a giggle
Orders a bowl of Frosted Flakes
Wakes up across from a few LA fakes
Eyeballs a piece of Chocolate Chip Crust
    French Toast
Best on the west coast

Doyle's ex lights up the town with her ugly
    LA frown
Doesn't have the beautiful inner crown
Not so funny comical lies sent him in reverse
Almost put him in a beat-up hearse

Wise with age to turn the second to last page
Got out from being engaged

Behind her backdrop of misery
She entered the Church doors
Tip toed down the aisle in a true June gloom
Doyle is blessed he's not the doomed groom
Or he'd be lying face down in his tomb

Sipping on a medium cherry Slurpee
Chewing on a piece of beef jerky
Doyle hits Highway 46 in his Dream 66
The unwed passenger seat sits a duffle bag full
    of cash
A yellow pack on the dash
Thankful to be thirty-five and Times Square alive
No need for the pedal to be on the metal

Doyle makes a pit stop for the coldest beer
    in town
Buys the local baseball caps an afternoon
    of rounds even the bar clown
But no one with an ugly frown

Staying Behind

Hammer stumbles back into his scene
Slowly hops on his Rusty Horse
Takes off like an out of control rocket
Into his dead end that won't ever end

Inside the deserted train station
He catches forty winks
Stolen from the devil on this unanswered
    earth
Once the color of a red orange sky
He misses her sunset eyes
Even her fairy-tale lies

She had Natalie Portman grace
Almost the same beautiful face
But on a damp overcast day
Shoved her way to the front of the empty
    ticket line
Bought a nonrefundable first class seat
    on a runaway meth train

Final destination unknown
Until buried four feet in defeat
She lies on the no view hillside
Above the burnt down filling station

Local flannels drinking their tasteless coffee
Expired licence plates cover the rusty walls
How many unbuckled rollercoaster rides traveled
    to reside here at the Broken Egg Café

Hammer tips the dreamless waitress
Walks passed the carved up wooden counter-top
Cheap tobacco follows him out the unlit
    emergency exit and into a 90's Tarantino take

Hammer drops a bicentennial quarter
    in the 40's out of order jukebox
Matches double whiskey shots
    with tomorrow's stool mate
Half buried in this no-name town
Their other half in the bar's closed down
    Lost and Found

Yet Hammer stays behind
Prays at every sundown for his honey bunny's
    sunset eyes to come back
    one more time to shine
Far away from that empty ticket line

Jen

Mom pours her morning tea
Lucky Charms for me
News and talk show host
    sits in the 24-inch Zenith
Brings extra color
With her All-American slice
    of apple pie spice

Ruffed up Tough Skins
And worn out Wallabies
Take me out the back screen door
Down the six chipped-up red brick steps
With an Olympic Gold Medal hurdle
Over my kid sister's annoying turtle
Early dude catches the fox
At the hopscotch box
I was ten and into Jen

Sitting side-by-side for the first time
Jen so studiously reading *Nancy Drew*
Me getting scolded by cigarette breath
Over-dressed librarian Mrs. Trotter
For imitating Vinny Barbarino from
    Welcome Back Kotter

Truckin' to the park pool
Being Fonzie cool
Hand in hand underwater
Shooting up like "Sky rockets in flight"
Our youthful "afternoon delight"

Some days we'd listen to KHJ
Wait for our special tune
Dance like we were bride and groom
Have fun with our Click Clacks
Crunching on orange Tic Tacs
A hero sub from Italia Deli
Jen made her peanut butter and jelly

TEN

Sat on the comfy cushy mustard yellow couch
Watched our favorite mouse
One hand on her light pink blouse
A few years later we'd hit the ceramic bong
Watch Cheech and Chong
Eat a box of Ding Dongs

Our youth is long gone
Jen and I now play Pong
And Donkey Kong with our teen
Quite the beauty queen
Even named after Norma Jean

The Sunday chirping choir missing
 a few high notes as I feed the mutts
Eat my bowl of Grape Nuts
Jane Pauley on the flat screen
Still brings her colorful All-American
 slice of apple pie spice

A Young Frankenstein
"Roll in ze hay" kind of day
Marvin Gaye's voice slowly fades
We Texas Two Step it
On the stone tile kitchen floor
Out our French doors
To appreciate our true romance and more

Jumping off an uncrowded Malibu Pier
A Bogey and Bacall together in one motion
Filling up on our 24/7 love potion
Splashing into the deep blue ocean

That's a Wrap

Sharon Stone played the character so well
He's not trying to dwell
But he got fooled taken to love school
A decade long run
Rubbing against scum
She keeps going back
To the same beat up drum
Mr. Scum

Lights camera action
She lied and lied again and again
And those non-Oscar performance cries
Take after take fake after fake
Give him a fucking break

Spends Devilish hours each day
On an 80's worn out casting couch
Rehearsing her played out untruthful dialogues
Needs to come up with new monologues

Hangs from a spineless vine
Not aging like a bottle of Italy's finest wine
Lack of grace non-genuine face
Zero glow to her narcissistic flow
Once slept with her beau's slimy bro
He'd rather walk across hot coal
Than be around a dried out soul

Free of her *Johnny Drama*
Happily alone in his Lucky Charm pajamas
"Frankly my dear I don't give a damn"

That's a wrap

Young Lies

Ray misses holding hands
And jumping in their hometown puddles
Doesn't miss the childhood struggles
Needs her warm hot chocolate mini
    marshmallows on top hearted cuddle
Another lonely ride in the darkness of an old
    Valley tunnel
Wishes he could explore his marriage fail
    in a therapeutic lifelong sail

A pack of Juicy Fruit in his back pocket
Ray walks into the vacancy for the loneliness
A Lebowski clone gives a graveyard shift groan
Rain drops dripping off Ray's out of tune
    69 Gibson guitar
Around the corner from the out of order
    ice machine
Their past -tale memories are tucked
    somewhere under the covers
The pain never went away when Mindy left on
    an unromantic 2 a.m. train

Four years to this lonesome Valentine's Day
All Ray has is her smiling face in a 3 by 5
    hearted frame

They honeymooned in Rome
Checked out Saint Peter's Dome
Held hands down the Tiber River
Had a Lady and The Tramp so in love spaghetti
    dinner
Recaptured their youth spending hours in
    a kissing booth
But a dark winding cobblestone road wore out
    each other's groove after misplacing their
    wedding shoes

Dylan lyrics and the love blues find their way
    through Room 9
The hard goodbye and empty bottles of 805's
    are close by the bedside

Ray draws the outdated curtains
Takes a swig of warm beer for the Valentine's
    Day lonely
His sleepless eyes watching Mindy's favorite
    romantic movie scenes passing by the
    Sea Shell Motel
And their young lies drifting into the early
    evening mist
Stopping in front of a precious little girl dressed
    like Dorothy Gale in ponytails
Hugging her yellow teddy bear
Mom and dad looking on with a North Star
    sparkle

Ray sits on the edge of the bed and tunes
    his guitar
Romantic thoughts begin strumming his and
    Mindy's wedding song
Feels her warm cuddles
Hears laughter in their hometown puddles

Sweet Time

Romance takes off higher than
   a Superman kite
Quickly nose-dives into a busy bee hive
You no longer feel alive at thirty-five
Back to the same local dive
Hearing the same old jive
Love stings don't go away
Maybe for a quarter of the day
You might be better off having flings
Than your heart being in a painful sling

Eating my bowl of Trix when I was six
Eyes glued to *Captain Kanagroo*
My sidekick Mandy Hicks
Ready to play some Pick-Up Sticks

Held hands as we got a bit older
Played backgammon on her back deck
With a mood ring tied around her neck
Said what the heck and gave Mandy a kiss

Right smack on those grape-flavored
Fun Dip lips with my hands around her hips
Listening to Gladys Knight & The Pips

Before sundown
Often strolled up to the horse trail
Me pulling on Mandy's pony tail
Hanging out under our special pepper tree
Pop Rocks in our demin jacket pockets
Slurping lime Otter Pops on cool fall breezes
Getting multiple brain freezes

Sunday nights
Plopping on tangerine colored bean bag chairs
Our mouths wide open
    tossing popcorn in the air
Watching TV's loving couple
Sonny and Cher

Smoking a Virginia Slim
Mandy's foxy mother blasting Linda Ronstadt
In the family's cool-looking sand tan Pacer
Turning the corners like my idol Speed Racer
Dropping us lovebirds at the Bob's Big Boy
Diving into a 'Silver Coblet' vanilla shake
And their famous hot fudge cake

Holding hands to Trigger Lake
Skipping our stupid Pet Rocks
When our navy blue Shell Toe Pro Keds
Arrived at the end of the abandoned dock
Making out and looking for Gazoo up in Mars
Between all those romantic teenage stars

Mandy was certainly a dandy
She was sweeter than lemon Pez candy
Now happily married to a dude named Randy
Me alone in a bar with my third brandy
Waiting on a midnight train to Georgia

Never think you're better than someone
but don't ever think you're less than anyone

NORTHRIDGE PARK

Welcomes You . . .

CITY OF LOS ANGELES - RECREATION & PARKS DEPARTMENT

Still Chasing

Their names still etched in stone
Between their childhood homes
Denny sees mom's tears again
Dripping off the dining room table
If only he borrowed Glenda's magic wand
His grade school crush would not be gone

Forever dressed in faded blue overalls
    with fudge pop in hand
Unlaced worn out black high tops skipping by
    the neighbors' heart-shape shrub
Across their front lawn just after dawn

Denny crosses the charmless boulevard
Once the dirt road to the funniest
TV couple's western ranch home
A discount shoe store shut the cinema's doors
But not on the classic movies and scenes
From the '70s silver screen
Paper Moon and Tatum O'Neal's
    Academy Award performance
Sits front and center in his buttered popcorn
    memory

Next to a broken payphone
Arby's signature sign stands alone
The local park sometimes after dark
Minus the cape was Denny's bat cave escape
His first French kiss and her strawberry blonde
 Farrah Fawcett feathered hair
Never left the closed down candy stand

Not so bright Friday night lights
Drunker than a skunk
Higher than two lost kites
No thought given to where
 his adult flight would land
Tuning out the number one
High School marching band
When smoking cloves
Underneath the grandstands

Bette Midler lyrics are still sound asleep
 inside the suffocating summer Valley air
A complicated heart waits at Bus Stop 242

For the ride to the Malibu side
Denny's only ride out tonight
    from this now no character town
A buck seventy-five
Alongside the depressing 405

A forgotten church but never alone
Listens in the teeter totter hours
    to a soulmate madness
Bell Tower speaks but has no place to be
Denny bums a smoke misses his own
She sips her morning high
They smell a romantic sunrise
The campus piano plays
Denny hears Mellencamp's cool voice
    through the bricks of Royce Hall
Old buildings never age
Like James Dean's last drag
Or Jean Harlow's last scene

Niagara Falls can't rinse off tomorrow's
    loneliness
Or today's brightless shadows on a parking
    structure that now stands
    adjacent to the outdoor mall
Where Denny met the one
Who was the most amusement park ride fun
Her adorable Ms. 'Queen City' face
In his reserved heart-shape space

Just a few thousand miles away
The birthday candles
    Denny and Scout share today
Will their birthday wish finally be the same
Still chasing her high after he dies

Empty

An off-the-wall kid
I spent most days smoking pot
Drinking soda pop behind the surf shop
No more carnival ride fun
Waking up to the depressed sun
Feeling like a box of empty Good & Plenty
Half my face smashed in the sand
Could use Grandma Josephine's loving hand
And the voices of the Allman Brothers Band

The mind should feel completely terrific
Staring out into the peaceful Pacific
But an unsweet salty taste
Bouncing off the broken down pier
Has Springsteen lyrics in my ears
Been in stripped gears for years
Never not in a deep mourn
Daily scars are torn and worn
Just once I wish I could toot my own horn

Came close to tasting wedding rice
Life's sugar and spice
Only if it's one hundred percent right
But a hometown inner demon
    hiding in a West Valley cubbyhole
At the last dysfunctional pay toll
Shot the tunnel light out twice
Sending me on a content ride back
On a death wish graveyard track

Dumped myself off on a barroom floor
Drinking alone with most of my own
Nowhere else for me to be free
Except maybe that pineapple underneath the sea

Slow Dancing Barefoot in the Cold Sand

Slow steps by my old elementary school
The side where we had Paper Drives
Black top is silent
Except the wind and Ann San Rio's silhouette
    jump roping through the trees
Next to where I learned to cross my t's
A young Ms. Leach in moccasins and
    bell bottom jeans
Our groovy first grade teach
Read *James and The Giant Peach*

Seeing weathered faces now in different places
A few have fallen from the Valley graces
Just yesterday we were laughing
Practicing tying our shoelaces
Running in three-legged relay races
Once kicked a ball over a backyard wall
Red Rover Red Rover send Ann San Rio
    right on over

Daydreaming on a forever date
Thru California's 126 and scenic Route 23
Feeling her sparkling elegant vibe
Riding shotgun in my '70 Vette ride
Holding hands humming to 'Van the Man'
Ann San Rio has a different kind of glow
More like an electrifying Broadway show

Over Malibu Seafood
A flock of seagulls
    gliding through their breeze
They stare without a care
As *Crash Into Me* by the Dave Matthews Band
Plays through the speakers of a candy
    red pickup truck
Me and Ann San Rio
Slow dancing barefoot in the cold sand
Having fallen in love tears
The lyrics and the ocean glare

Flowing through her beautiful auburn hair
Knows she's the only one on my love list
The way I kiss her in the shoreline mist

A drizzly Honeymoon night outside the
    Frosty Queen
Sharing a soft serve ice cream and
    a plastic spoon
Looking into her Olivia Wilde eyes
For the next nine lives
Ann San Rio daydreams always end
With a romantic line from a movie scene

The chain-linked fence
    in front of the kindergarten yard
Where I received my first Valentine's card
The words "Be Kind" written with Dixie cups
And two hearts outlined in cherry sweet tarts

Arriving back to my pal Pops McGruder's
Diving into the unheated swimming pool
Numbing my unsweetened youth for good
Excluding the days of Doorbell Ditch
Skipping Mass
Playing Snake in the Grass
And Tap-Tap-Tap in our 501's and Vans

At 2
cuddles with
WINNIE THE
POOH

At 4
can't open the
DOOR

At 11
thinks of
HEAVEN

At 16
not so
SWEET

At 17
homecoming
QUEEN

At 20
still watching
BUGS BUNNY

At 26
back on the
FIX

At 29
continues the
rollercoaster
RIDE

At 32
nothing
NEW

At 34
kicks down
that
DOOR

At 35
feeling semi
ALIVE

At 36
therapy for
all life's
LICKS

At 38
forever date
with best
friend
TATE

NEVER
too late to
find your
FATE

ABUSE
gets no
TRUCE

True Friends Are Like Stars.
You Can Only Recognize Them
When It's Dark Around You . . .

—Bob Marley

Early dude catches the word

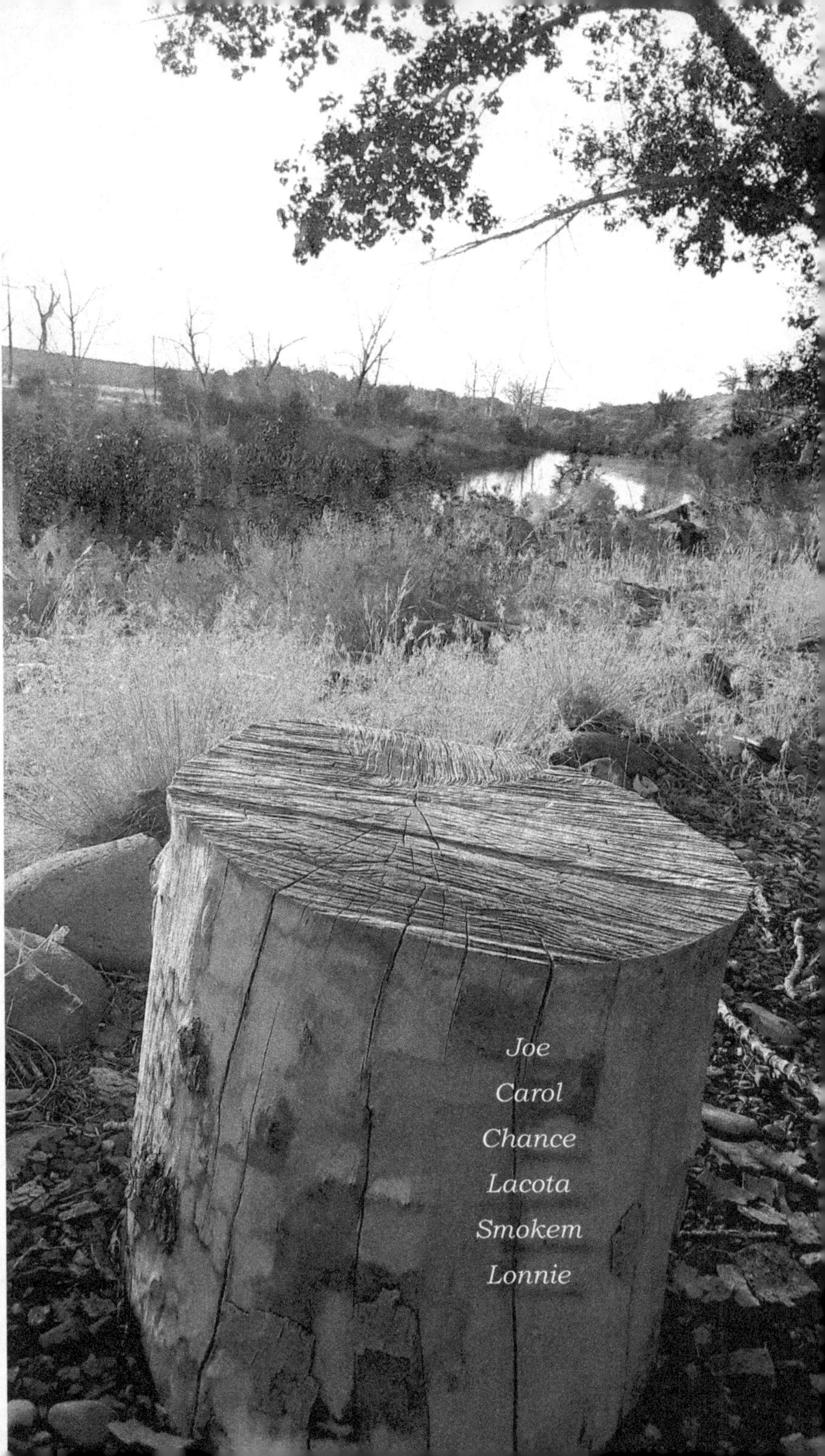
Joe
Carol
Chance
Lacota
Smokem
Lonnie

Acknowledgments

My 'Rugrats' for always keeping me in check

Karen Mumaw

Lisa Finn

Em Gem

Betty Sue

Holly Cantos

Derv and Krisi

Tim 'Diego' Lane

Anthony Acampora

Mikey D

Rail

Aunt Joan

G.B. and Cathy

Jeff 'Manny' Gelb

Jo Jo Jolene

Timmy K

Ms. Kemp (High School English/Writing Teacher)

Jackie Lennon

Tony 'Morty' Mortillaro, 52 years of friendship

Devon Pennsteen

Susan Shankin

Pleasants

Diana and Suzy

The late Chris McCandless and the late Luke Perry

LSU campus and 'Mike The Tiger'

UCLA campus

Oregon City

Mighty Carson River

Lucy Crebs

Asada El Inferno Taco Stand, Reseda Blvd/Plummer St

Northridge Park (Annie, Kadeem, Parv, and Zayne)

Oakridge Estate Park

Spicy Mango Margaritas (served by Ms. Azteca)

Vanalden Avenue

Minor League Baseball

Atomic Fire Balls

LSU Bus Stop

CAR WASH ❯

About the Author

Author photo by Jack Fennessy

Robert Sparago was born in New York City. In 1970, at the age of 5, he moved to Northridge, CA (a suburb in the San Fernando Valley) where orange and pepper tree groves and ranches were rapidly replaced by never-ending tract homes. As the years marched on, Northridge formed its layers—decent hard-working middle-class families, team sports, family dysfunction, the entertainment industry, and the Valley's burgeoning drug culture all created a backdrop for Robbie's adolescence.

As an adult, Robbie had his share of trials and tribulations, both personal and professional, including bouts of depression.

On June 6, 2019, he finally cut all ties from dysfunction and psychological hardships and set out on a therapeutic odyssey on the road. Robbie traveled across the country—mostly by bus—to become an older, more civilized version of the late Chris McCandless, whose life was popularized by author John Krakauer.

After meeting up with a childhood friend at their old stomping ground, Northridge Park, Robbie reflected on the day and wrote, *Still Chasing.* While living on a friend's farm in Oregon, he continued to express himself through words.

The result is this collection.

Armed with uncanny recall and a unique twist on reality, Robbie has the ability to capture the ghosts from his past and share it with the world. He can instantly create a sense of longing that most of us know intimately. The rest is a soul-stirring collection of personal reflections that are raw and real at times, nostalgic and playful at others.

Part poetry, part song lyric, part personal prose, part good old fashion storytelling . . . each entry feels like a short film you want to watch over and over again.

Surprisingly, underneath the pain and heartache, there is a joy, a love for unique experiences, and a devotion to the people and places we spend time with while passing through this relentless condition called life.

For feedback or questions, contact the author at: robsunsetinthemorning@gmail.com

www.ingramcontent.com/pod-product-compliance
Lightning Source LLC
Chambersburg PA
CBHW031527040426
42445CB00009B/426